Prayershreds

Prayershreds

poems

Bruce Beasley

ORISON
BOOKS

ISBN: 978-1-949039-41-2

Orison Books
PO Box 8385
Asheville, NC 28814
www.orisonbooks.com

Distributed to the trade by Itasca Books
(952) 223-8373 / orders@itascabooks.com

Cover art: "Fish in termite eaten book" by Rosamond Purcell.
Used by permission of the artist.

Image on p. 35: "Tenacity" (bronze sculpture, 1990) by Bruce Beasley.
Used by permission of the artist.
www.brucebeasley.com

Manufactured in the U.S.A.

ORISON
BOOKS

CONTENTS

I

II

III

for Suzanne and Jin
my prayers that can never be torn

For what, again, shall I sing hymn? For things Thou hast made, or things Thou has not? For things Thou hast made manifest, or things Thou has concealed?

—Corpus Hermeticum

Self-Portrait

I am words in a language I don't speak

a dead one

Are
they even words? I've never seen
them carved on any stele unearthed

slashes scorch marks red
ocher months-dried reed

funerary

Never heard
that throat-trill
anywhere else

fricative like the spill
of candle wax over ice

I don't think anyone
ever spoke it

Does it have
an alphabet
or assemblage of
learnable runes

Is that sound the talonprint of an owl

I'm translating into English even now

Burnt and pictosyllabic
stalactite-lit

How do you say in this dead language *Hello*
How do you say *How many days' walk are you*
(whoever you are)
How many days' walk are you

away

3

Rite

Is It taking again its holy orders.

(It is known by the alias
of It,
abstemious of name.)

Candlesticks, linens, spilt vials.

Overtipped candlesticks, scorchmarked shrouds.

Approach It with appropriate fits of trembling.

*

Would it be seemly
even now
to genuflect or kneel, smear chrism
or ashes, recite

to It the Pater Noster

It may have forgotten, or expunged
selections from the Book of Hours, those
hours already
taken down.

*

Sickles, scrolls, censers, scales.
For a time, and a time (Art

4

wast shall
be) and time

no more. Shall we
drape our faces, rend our garments, and inquire,

as several seals remain yet intact,
what might be—to our avail—still
supplicatable?

Loathsome Repetitions

It is with great delight and regret I come
to bear unto you

the word *battology*, meaning
"the wearying repetition of a word."

"Battologies of loathsome repetitions," quoth the OED.
"When we pray, let us not battologize."

Let us not battologize but alter
the wounded text
with corrections:

For *absolutely* read
Not so fast.
For *what do you want* replace throughout
Why do you even want.

For *erotic* say *erratum.*
For *erratum* say *exactly as intended.*

I will never say the word *battology* aloud.
How long has it now been
since anyone has? Don't you, should you read this, let
its four syllables so much as dry your tongue.

Battologize at your own reckless risk.

Reckless should have been written above as *wreckless*.

For *at your own wreckless risk*, read *I dare you*.
For *I will never say the word* battology *aloud*
read *I have not ceased to battologize, loathsomely, that word;*
its breath has—every second I've been speaking now in writing out to you—
never failed to dry my tongue.
This is my error-riddled supplication. Take it as a talisman, an apotropaic fetish,
an act of idolodulia.

(Battologize *idolodulia* x 5.)

For *When we pray, let us not battologize*, close your eyes and join with me in prayer:
I cried unto the Lord with my voice;
with my voice unto the Lord did I make
my supplication
Did I make my wrecked and dry-tongued supplication
Did I make my supplication Lord unto thy voice
Into thy voice
Overspeaking and contradicting thy voice

For *supplicate* the correct text would be *Pour out my troubles*.
For *poured out my complaint* the proper version
to be inserted is *shedded out my prayer*.
For *shedded out my prayer* read *prayershreds,*

read *tell him all my problems*, read גָאֶשְׁפֹּךְ לְפָנָיו שִׂיחֲי צָרָתִי לְפָּנָיו אַגִּיד:
For *read*, substitute *supplicate*.
For *Refuge failed me, no man cared for my soul*
please use corrected text
My soul is like earth without water for Thee.

My soul is like earth without water for Thee.
My soul is like earth without water for Thee.
My soul is like earth without water for Thee.

Outside the Realm of Unconcealment

Was I in the past? Was I not in the past? What was I in the past? How was I in the past? Having been what, what did I become in the past? Shall I be in the future? Shall I not be in the future? What shall I be in the future? How shall I be in the future? Having been what, what shall I become in the future? Am I? Am I not? What am I? How am I? Where has this being come from? Where will it go?
　　　　—**The 16 Imponderable Questions, from the *Suttasava Sutta***

Does the virus have a soul?
　　　　—**Luther Allen**

I

Undoubtedly the virus has a soul,
acquisitive, invasive, self-
replicative

in the image and likeness of our own:
as the Buddha says of us, *All
I-making and mine-making.*

II

The name of God is Gott. Jesus's name
is Yeshua. And lo they shall call

His name Emmanuel. God-with-Us. Call
His name Omega, Alpha. The name of God is Bog.

The name of God is Бог.
The name of God

is God, the heretic Name Worshippers
on Mount Athos preached. God is

the utterance of the name of God, systole- and diastole-synchronized on the
      breath.
Shout it morning and night in convulsions of ecstasy.

III

Doubtless depermitted during quarantine eye-

contact's microexpressive
intimations of concealed
concern or pleasure, denied their transmutations

into words that quiver in molecules wine-tannic on the air
between us,
I've taken my hand drill's whinesqueal to the doorjam.
Like the Russian "Hole Worshippers" who carved into their huts
a deep and narrow fissure { }
and prayed each day into its visibly
empty substitute for the Orthodox god
they no longer believed in,
 "My house, my hole, do save me!"

I pull down my facemask, puff up my breath, and call out into my crumbling
      bore-hole
the manifold names of house gods
(Limentinus of the threshold,
Umbrae of the shadows of the dead)

O sacred house
O sacred hole

Self-
exilic in unexodus, in this
much-disinfected, restranged home.

IV

It's *madness and vexation:* the Buddha says
only those can come
from haranguing with the 16 Imponderable Questions

but they are most of what I want to know.

Asylee at the oracle, scrutatorial, with:
Is the soul of the virus immortal? Did
it put on our knowledge with our power?
Having been *what*, what
will it become?

What? ("All men say 'What'
to me," Dickinson wrote, "but I thought it a Fashion—")

Moot the question.

So the Buddha repelled Malukyaputta's inquiries
Is the body the soul? Is the cosmos eternal?
Where after death will the Buddha *be?*
There still is death and birth and lamentation,
he said, whether or not the Self is the same as the body,
whether or not the cosmos is mortal like us.

—Whether or not the virus
in us, I'd add, is mortal
like us; whether or not the virus in us *is* us.

V

But did they ever, lo—
(the name appears only once in the whole New Testament)—
really call His name Emmanuel?

VI

I type into a chatbot Heidegger's question:

Are what is past and future also present
outside the realm of unconcealment?

It answers: **'What' is a word to ask questions.**

That WAS a question, I—in the cramped chat window—bicker back.

Ask me again in a different way please.
Are the past and future also present?
The what?

VII

Mystic means to close the lips and eyes. Say
'what' to me, Christos, Tetragrammaton, Dieu,
Lord Emmanuel,
woodchip-clogged 3/16"
drill-hole,

if, without offending, I might ask.

And Though This World Should Threaten to Undo

Language being
a torn hymnal, ripped sheet
music and severed words like deus
noster refugium
blown sideways from one another in an open window's draft and away

Metaphor being eighth-
notes clung together by a top-bar half-beat each and loosened

off their syllables like

C

dost ask who Christ is   He   that Jesus may it be

D7   G

All grasping at some otherness an unwritten language's scribbles a note a
        chord a crotchet
octaves ascending   the scale
As hymnwords are to organ keys as

hymen is to hymn's
glottal stop mid-*wit-*

ness

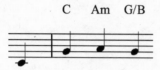

Some snag of sound on meaning, some score for prayer, some initial clef or cleft

The sacred's
fracture

lo, his doom is   sure;   one lit - tle word shall fell___ him.

into Thing Itself and its
arcane similitudes, metaphor
being what it is, a darkly glass,

melted-bronze mirror dimly polished

with scrub sponge and pumice,
an enigma a darke
speakyng

—Know me
face to face,
even as You shall be also known:
darkly, fully.
Language
being what it is, 44
phonemes disattached and scrambled and strung
into the hard psalm-music of *help thou* and *Out of the depths* and *with devils*
        filled and *O*

Gather the scattered

psalms and indulgences of scourge
for the hungering
rearrangements of the flesh

for the hungering reassembly of vehicle and tenor,
scribbled note and sung one—

Let's collaborate
on a new arrangement of A Mighty Fortress Is Our God
scored for linguolabial trill

and Holy Ghost

our ancient foe   doth seek to work us woe

Work us
(backslid and thrice-relapsed)
but work us weal, Your Mighty Highness, sight-sing
me bar by bar, sharp and flat, tempo maestoso, slower and slow and sola fide

(Language and metaphor blessed
estrangements)

Falsetto solo for Sinner-
Regardless-of-What, bassoon
accompaniment for the lowest
tones of the sacred crack
These
be our duet sheet
music tears

for our dissonant
final arrangements

Easterwards

Have ye here any meat

Honeycomb and broiled fish, vinegar-sponge

Children, have ye any meat

Bread crust broken he who dips
must be delivered   into the hands
Except I shall see in his hands the print
of the nails
why seek ye   among the dead
the living

spices and ointments smite their breasts

Children, have ye any meat
Feed my lambs
Feed my sheep

Art thou only a stranger
in Jerusalem   Early at the sepulcher
and sore afraid

draws near   what has come to pass
temple's scrim ripped   holy of holies

em   mb
     ptyto

          it behooved
          Chr   ist   to

suf
    fer
to suffice

supplicant at the sepulcher craved the body of Jesus he is not
here

He breathed on them
Sufflations of the holy ghost
Suffer the children Children, have ye
any meat

mortal and reembryal
burnt horizon ri
sen
upbraid
their unbelief
He is not here   must be delivered

rizon
blaze at sunrise
hor
seven devils cast

linenwrapped
What manner of communications *are* these   They shall speak
with new tongues
linaments
unguents
         anointed of the lingual

           The Word   witness wit
           less

para   dice dox
paradisewards today you will

be with me

Why are you weeping touch me not

rood's blood
sepulcher's
pulchritude

into the hand
nigh at hand
Children, have ye any meat? Cast
and the nets strained
and the lines groaned with fish-
catch into the hands
Children, have ye so little
faith so little
meat   Hand-

le me, and see

Last Supper with Halibut and Maledictions

That a scripture might be written in an ink
squeezed from a seaweed's green
in lines along the skin and flesh-folds
of halibut

Woes and curses blurred
a little by its oils
Chopped stalks of lemongrass punctuating
its opaque striations and the flash-

frozen flakes crumbling with the crushed
garlic and cold
Pacific saltwater sealed into its skin,

a stanza, pan-seared
in
and tasting of jeremiad and vilification

and benedictions of ginger strips
I am weary of repenting

saith the Lord
I will cause to cease the voice of mirth the voice
of gladness   I will make
thee a burnt mountain
thou shalt be desolate forever

the harvest is passed
the summer is ended   and we are not
saved

—And offered,
as in the dream it was,
as a temporal sacrament, that its languaged

flesh be taken in as sustenance
and as riddance
This is my body, that

having tasted of its sweetened malediction
we need never render again
what that
seared flesh once read

Ars Poetica

Blood spheres and pomegranate seeds I lay down
on your unfrequented
weed-snarled and barbed-
wire sequestered altar

Did you know I'd be back so soon

with four spits in each cardinal direction

four for each cardinal number and four for each cardinal
sign
Capricorn Libra solstice-openers

and forty hard exhalations, each bearing

a phoneme (some of them a syllable
some of them a word),
some laden with mown-
grass scent

of chopped dandelion stems and mint

How many times now did I

give you knuckle-scab and nape's sweatslick,
ex voto snatches of dream with their ripped sleeves
when they got away

Did I bring you immolations of
exaugurate
imprecate

mysterianist
re-bless

re-blest torch-ash

Can it ever be enough

Chrism of balsam
offeratory of this ripped
strand

of lawn-length spiderweb invisible except
when wind divides the cumulonimbi and sprung-loose sun

divulges the high thin filament's sporadic downline dazzle

The Paradox of the Heap, in Heraclitus's River

If this is what I give you, made of air-
through-throat and made of thought-

shoved-into-thought the way
a river *is* the press

of its water on its water, step again
into the silt-crumb of sediment

inrunneled in mouthward
involutions through the dry-

ridged bedform,
deposition of all

its flowing's
leavings.

*

If this is what I give you, made of what's meant,
a heap in just a word, the two

syllables of *river*
in a stream's lieu. If I give you parch

of riverbed where an anthill
just stomped down is hauled

antload by antload off
till it's no more

a mound and still a form
reminiscent of the mound

and of the boot that crushed it, a trillion grains
that gave up being grains to make these

arched vestibules for the brood
and sidebranchings of fungus gardens,

souvenirs of structure that remind
what order might have meant, pheromone trails

leading back inside the smushed-in chambers,
shed wings left there on the midden heap.

*

These are the deictics, the *this* and the *that*.
These syllables, that anthill, this river

ridged and rigid with its unflux.
That ant, the one whose mandibles

hoist away the single grain
that pushes its anthill over

from *heap*
to heap-no-more.

*

Can a river still be known
as a river when all its water has left?

Step in again, and see, as into *this*, if this
is no more than strokes and ovals anymore,

ink-dry-on-cream-emboss, shapes
that gave up being syllables, words and lines, anthills and rivers, if this were

—it is—what I have
to give you, decohering slowly on both our tongues.

*

The logic of the paradox says: subtract a grain
from a trillion-grained heap and it remains a heap—

take two away, then a thousand, then a trillion-minus-one
(because where exactly does the mound divest

itself of moundedness) and the last
granule should be itself a heap

still, a singularity, a colony,
the meaning of multiplicity pressed in a single speck.

Disconnected Limbs Wandered Seeking Everywhere for Union

Empedocles claimed that in the distant past . . . single parts of animals arose separate from each other. Heads without necks rolled pathetically around in the environment, trying to survive. Arms, legs, spleens, and eyes presumably crawled the earth in a grotesque parade. Occasionally these organs and limbs accidentally clumped together and managed to survive for a short time.
    –Stephen Asma, *On Monsters*

For even as they [Strife and Love] were aforetime, so too they shall be; nor ever, methinks, will boundless time be emptied of that pair.
    –Empedocles, fragment 166c

```
                    verge
                    vir urge  e ve merge vemerge virurge  gorge a
                    rose er  roserosar     y se
                    er        searsere

                    searose arkdark
               ashwash downdrown un
                           do
                    who eroser roarribcry
```

```
se mer sea meremar
y
chi mer a kai
ros ba al de us
me du
sa
the o ma chi
```

for mal
chas mal
mal form fic
tile fi ckle ca
vern ous ve
nus ni
                    hi lo

---

                    de-
luge loosespume   bloomgloom lurksuck lotic
                    lot
                    us
                    leafgnaw

om phal lus   be
leave eve
grieve fe
cund par
tum un
der sod
shun belle

---

                                        ble bi ba
                                        bel la bi
                                        al

bibile sinfangled angerfanged   dog ma
                                        tic
                                            shun
                                        dic
                                            tion

                                        flay mis
                                        dys
                                        schism

---

        doom salt psalt er sod
        om

---

mur mur der mur   der or der cry chi di
es chasm   clysm clit
or al lit   tor al tore all al pha phi
lo so phy so phi   a mons ven
er is mon   ster

vir a   gin ous
mens   is mind

mar   ry vir
gin vag   in
a scen   si on scion
ac sea   dent more birth mor dent
her o ni   hi lo gy no
airsearthrueruth rood birth er upting earthsurge a rose a rose

Urnburn, alit. Spurn   birth. Bear
all, bur   i al.

```
              del                                              sybil
                phi                                        ble
              in                                         la
              fi                                        syl
                del                              ave
                  de              clovelove
                      pray prave
                  truth          cli
                ruth               tor
              less                  is
              or a                    scrip
            pray or                     rip
          a cle                           ture


              _____


            sci                                        ence
            ark                                      skyarch
          archi                                    me dies screw lev
            er leave her                           enmaled quark
                ex pire                            a ment
                  quan                             ti
                    fy          sin e
                      qua
                      non
                      gon-
                      -gony
                      ca te
                      chism
                      schism


              _____
```

$$\Omega$$

```
        bel                 bellig
       erent               slay a
        bel              mal male
         core              rupt
    w ife str ife       strovelove
            co it     us
                    en
                    ter
                    in to
                    her

                    inter
```

Male dic tion?
        Urgescourge. Lot-loathe.
Looselouche?
        Ash-am. Ash shamed.
Unclothed? Loinloathed?
        Dirge de-urge. Nym phal. He lix.
Updove?
        Dovedown. Flume.
Burgeonpurge?
        Fallow fall o pi an. New fall. De ark. Evesieve. Scyther.
Fiat felix? Fiat licks?
        Darkle. Noxlust. Wrathturerupture. Incor ri gi ble suc
        cor. Lustloose. Phal lust.
Know edge?
        No. Gorge. Araratwrath. Gor gon. Know no knowgnaw.
        Cephalic. Menmind.
Her o? Hier o?

Num i nous. Numb in us. Spir it ex spire. Depyre. Kneel
to nihil.

So lo her lyre
strum purepyre
ci pher pi
pa gan mu
sics con soul an
them an a
them a

Downwash over earthsurge, de-   luge   Dove-drown over Ararat
        silverwashed plumes ripped

                        loose by seaspume

|Charybdis sucks| |Scylla lurks|

|the dark mael strom| |in vi si ble in her cavernous|

|down| |lair |
            lair down lay her down
                 a vern us

ryb Dis   la Syl
        —Disribbed; lascivious

                    Sigh
              no more la

dies   di es
irae:

–Scry
from Delphi's
earthmouth, gnawed laurel leaves, pneuma
from the chasm, wrath of incohering, hug
to that noxious, bituminous
crag

–Scy-
la, six-dogged and loin-
fanged, six-mouthed
Skyllo: to rend. Hug
hard by her less mortal
crag

–Sci-
ence, rend, di-
vide, cleave,
for know-
ledge, hug its slashing
crag

Numbered numbered di
vided Mene mene tekel upharsin
Measured, mensural, found
wanting, found to want

Failed-male. Mal-male. *A woman is
a mutilated male*, the Teacher teaches.
So sci- ence begins.
The catamenia, he says, *are semen*

*only not pure, not in them
the soul.*
A woman is an infertile male,
he says. De-

formed, misbirthed. Scat,
scat, scatterscathe, lyrely. Men ses se men mene mene
te kel up har sin.
Fe cund de

fuck fe lare
to suckle fe

tal fe tor in
felix culpa de

        male vul
        va e volve
        evolve evulve e
        volve

        Wrathiraepray.

Women's birth would be an accident,
such as that of other monsters, says
On Truth.

To know
would be to rend, sci-
sile. Eve
and Mary, ScyllaChimera, pray for
us, who live
from fuck to fuck. Wife-
of-Lot, in the hour
of our living on, pray for us, salt our earth.

Bruce Beasley
Tenacity
(1990)

Not Easily Pulled Asunder

for Bruce Beasley the sculptor: Ten for his *Tenacity*

Sculptors are poets of shape.   *Poets are syllable-sculptors.*
        –Bruce Beasley   **–Bruce Beasley**

. . . where I am indivisibly this and *that; where I experience the other in myself and the other-than-myself experiences me.*
        –Carl Jung

I

Say there's a self split open
by what wants

out of it
(its insularity), and

the break's unclean:
cast bronze cast out of the globe

of itself, in mottled-
gray excrescent

rhomboids, the sphere's
insides gone angular and stabbed

out of the fissure
their emergence keeps

forcing farther apart.
Their eruptive faces stay

interred in the bronze
of each other—intermelded polyhedra

seceding from cubes' secession
from the sphere-surface's umber sheen:

and each partakes a little of the sphere's
ruptured curve,

juts rounded into wide arcs, and triangles
burst from the cut–

into in-
sides of the sphere, which

ought, being elliptical, to have nothing
to do with sides. Solid bodies

made, by the shapes
invisibly inscribed within them, to alter

their very nature just to hack their own forms loose.

II

When you gave me your spare
left thumb, Bruce, I had to find
some way to stitch it in

to sinew and wrist-artery
just where the crosshatched
lifeline hits a scraggled *X*. I had

to finger the numb, the sallow
offsize of it, to trace with my other thumbs
its new crowding on my palm, brush

its chisel-dust, and teach
the antibodies that it belonged
to us.

III

They used to say *nomina numina*,
names are numinous, they used

its substitutable vowels as their song
of what the spelled could do. They used

to say *nomen est omen*, the name's an omen,
the consonant-shed

unveiling the oracle's temple
just inside the word.

They used to believe in a name
not as arbitrary but as ominous,

omenous, *us*, the appellation
a rattleboned talisman you could shake

at a thing enough
and it would warp itself to become

what we called it.
We squeeze our way out of the rent

hemispheres of our same
name, Bruce, and there I find you drawn

to the shapes of paradox
as much as I am, Homonym, its

duplicity, simultaneous curve and jab.
Your vocabulary, you say, is shape and emptiness.

So's mine: a scribble and a stroke
and left-white, then little

vowel-quaver, silence-quiver,
the said, the unsaid, and flitting

among them the meant, and what
it never meant
to mean, to turn
away from, or

into.

IV

Summer's last cherry tomatoes, deep-hung in their trellis-cage
and split down the middle from over-
ripeness and rain-glut, gold
seed-ooze through the ripped
flaps of peel, their stems
burst out through the air-sphere
of a swarm of gnats

that want back in.

V

"Resemblance
is just the truth's skin," you say:

you want shape
without imitation, emotion
"without representing
any recognizable object"—

Shape, you say's "a mute
and articulate language" of its own.

Still these tacit, tactile
shapes of yours before me
are like

a metaphor

for metaphor: secretly
similar interpenetrating
unalikes—
smoothed cube, sawn-
into-slices sphere—*this*
obliquely intercutting alien *that,*

this and *that* flashing
their heretofore unseen resemblance—

Metaphor's semblances are
vertebrae and viscera, not
the skin, structures
of some
unrecognizable underform,
penetralium's expulsion like

yours, and mine, and our dis-
resemblance, and the like,
and the like,

and the like.

VI

So which are you, which am I:

define, or
to set forth the meaning of—

definiendum,
that is, or
definiens, the word
defined, or the ones
we need to know already to define them?

VII

By *cube* shall we mean a thing
with six faces, each staring
at its opposing identical
other, or one
multiplied and multiplied
by some figure of itself?

‡

To be "normal" geometrically is to be
perpendicular, "right"-
angled, barely

to intersect.

‡

What keeps a sphere
from being a circle, that's what
keeps you and me
obliquely
parallel, keeps us

on two
different-dimensional planes
(shape's syntax, syllables'
interstabbable shapes),

each's selfhood
ex-dwelling, in-
pressed—
tenacious, that is, meaning
not easily
pulled asunder.

VIII

These surfaces—you say which ones I mean—can't hold themselves

apart:
doppelgangers,
doublewalkers,
oval and edge.

Ø

Figures of shape, or speech: many-faced, much-jutted.

Ø

Every point on a sphere's surface is called
umbilical, and means to hold
to itself
the self that comes from in it.

Ø

Doppleganger, why are you
going
outside me.

Ø

A sphere's got no face

but also, no place that could slit.

IX

I'll play
the failing inhibitions of the sphere
that wanted only to hold everything inside

at perfectly measured equidistance from surface to core;

you play the cuboids' defection, spearheads
prying the hidden open to the eye, its smooth
unhatched inner self.

I'm talking about what I think
you're talking about,
the shapes of self-concealment, their

hypotenuse and circumference and obtuse
angles, the depths that won't stay put inside the surface,
the surface disguising itself
as revealed depth, the postulates

we tell ourselves
are self-evident, so that
we may not ever find out
otherwise.

X

I'm learning Korean. There's a consonant shape
like an egg balanced on its end

O

that stands for nothing, makes no sound:

just the pretense of a consonant
a syllable needs
to get started sometimes, since vowel-
voices aren't allowed to come first.

You say its name EE-oong, though that's
all the voice it's got: alias
for what's unsoundable, ovoid
out of which come bursting

the jagged shapes that make their ruptive way.

Verily

I

Shut your eyes—we were taught
in the Children's Sermon
on how to pray—
shut your eyes tight until
you hear the pastor say *Amen*

but sometimes when I forgot to listen

for that end-signal word, sleep and prayer
would indistinguish themselves

II

Mandatory postrequisite
of creed
prerequisite for exit *Amen*

Vocally italicized *Yes*

that compelled and terminal
assent

It means *Verily, so be it, decidedly it's true,*
means *Here is where we go
back to normal-talk*

We make it
mean

Please Lord let it end make it
mean *Oh God*
would would would
that it were so

III

To my body I will be as the
amen
is to the flesh's
Let us pray Let us pray Let us pray

IV

Every amen
scissors the traced
outline of the prayer, ripping
the cut-out space of what we say to God

from the scrapped
silver silk of all we'd never say

Aria

–Ecclesiastes 1:6

Blessed we
who hanker
after air

Our mouths will fill

again again with what we tongue-
and inner-cheek-mould
it into

Syllable-coalescences
Alphabets named for what

alphas and betas compose them:
ordinal ordained and spirit-breathed and literal

—Meaning-born and -bearing, like sung
lyrics as they're threshed

off music with a flail
a flagellum and hurled
to be winnowed
by the wind—what's
chaff what's flesh what the
saved

grain its dropped
seed   A word

I need a word with you

When the wind bears away the melodious
air
virginal harpsichordal
O Lord I need with you a winnowed

word Not that
departed
deconsonanted devowelled and
utterless blown air

Will

Want; don't.
Wouldn't, did, as spume's
throughswell into slabs'
looseheaped jetty fissures.

Must; can't.
Oughtn't; will, as a breakwater's
broken granites
enable a tidepool's
agitated self-protectiveness,
crouch under crash.

Wall; will.
Stall; call, as surge-shake
and downheave
let flow over seariven pilestone.

Strove-for; staved-
off. Spurn; gush, as
the stasis of the isolate's
reviolable harbor, swabscrub
cove to runnel's inrush
bruntslosh into seawall groyne.

Hinder; enter. In-
hibit; inhabit, as
seaload's sandblast
occupies and redefines
tide pool's hesitant and semipaused
saltwater glint and noon-sun
shiver.

Guarded; God-
smite and billow-spew
into breaker-sheltered
refuge; poised; Op-
pose our sopor
and our hankering.
Languor; lust. Urge; urn.
Refuse; re-fuse, as in

unbreach and smash-merge back together
shelter and welter, haven;
haven, Lord, wilt
thou will to shelter
us, heave us back to place.

Dogstarred

Seam-fray off phlox & dry hollyhocks

Steam spray
from hosed
hot sidewalks
& hiss

Smokesmited
sky
unsolsticed un-
sanctioned unchanged

Steeple-shadow like
a scorchmark on pavement
droughtscar doubtsmolder

Unsummonable Summa

Asymptomatic
these summer days sick
anyway stainsamed
simulacrum
of unseen unseeable omnium dis-
ease

Solaceless
reign of unrain
Unquenched corona
Simulated unstimulated
some unnamable seeming

Steaming
undersmush of
smoked-out sun
stuckstruck

Sirius dogstar
semblances of mystic/
mythic
resemblances
Call
off your dog Orion hazed
& dissembling

desymboling August moon
mon semblable
mon semblable blasé

& blah'd away sine qua
non
sun-stunned & samemaimed
plagued and wildfire-rained and decades-long war
surrendered and faces re-mask-choked

chokechained Sirius's singed & dog & doggéd song-

stifled days

stay

By the Road of By and By

. . . we get to the house of Never.
–proverb

Siamo smariti, we said, in what
Italian we knew from Dante, *we're lost*,
on the hillroad to Settignano.
Umbrella pines shielding us from dusklight,
we banged the iron door-knocker cross
at a convent, the only house we could find.
The little nun tried to hide
her smirk at our garbled *Inferno*-speech.
Lost like "in perdition."
Perchè la diritta via era smarita.
Because the true way/
right road/unstraying/
straightforward pathway,
was missing, lost. Bewildered.
She crossed herself and giggled.
House of Now, who goes there, who lives
inside your locked mansion, and how did they get through your marble door?

*

I have followed premeditation's
downcoiling hell-road,
its paving stones of good intentions,
through Time, knowing,
I knew, the straightway, the sweet
by and by—have swayed
on wavelashed, frayed-rope suspension
bridges, crossed and crossed those bridges though they never

came, will never come.
As it *were*, the saying goes. Past,
subjunctive: is always *were*. Time
covers and *dis*covers everything, they say, but who

says Time will tell us anything? And when?
Inflected,
-fected, as though the verbs
were to tell us nothing
of time and its insistent
illusion. The tense
will always have been present.

*

A *by-your-leave* is an apology
for not having sought
permission. By-your-leave, Time, I have left
along the road of by and by, over
treacherous and elusive bridges, toward
Never's stable trough.

*

Siamo smariti, we're lost, we've been
lost, we will have been
lost, where are we
bound that could be
perdurable?
Tell Time you've seen through to its stitches, their dis-
covered scarifying
sutures and never-snipped-

off threads. Tell Time you know how
cut it's been—the bloodbunched
pucker of its skin—and how
haphazardly it's now bound
around the scar.

*

Give Time time:

The Saying's no
sooner said than
it dissipates on air

to cochlea-quiver
on inner ear's cilia and bony labyrinth
and, brain-deep, shocks its way
through tens of

thousands of neurons
into temporal lobe, to ask itself

what could it mean: *Give Time time?*

Of what else, but flux and entropy
and gravity-warp, is Time made?
Time's got all the time there ever was,
including all that's lost, as it
were and is, *smarito.*
What could the proverb mean:
Time is an inaudible file?
I hear its grate-rasp, scratch-grind,
inside every word.

Called to Lapse

And straightway the father of the child cried out, and said with tears,
Lord, I believe; help thou mine unbelief.
–Mark 9:24

Let us turn now to the passages on Unbelieving:

502.1 through 503.5 in this marred
thesaurus, long half-de-spined, backcoverless, to its much-used
vocabularium of apostasy and *o ye of little faith.*

502.1

I admit, Lord, I have told these words like a rosary.

Tongued delicately the syllables of *dubiety* and *qualm.*
Proclaimed by heart the verses and chapters
of *set no store by* and *undeludable.*

Often I have drowsed on the chill wet
crabgrasses of Gethsemene, while Judas stirred
and some carpenter rose before dawn to fulfill
an urgent new order for a cross.
Often I've half-heard through some inchoate dream your
Sleepest thou? Couldest thou not watch with me one hour?

502.2

My dog Beauregard walked each day the length of his long untangleable
tether:
left yard azalea, sidewalk-border to stone bench, backyard thorn bush.
When once I forgot to attach his collar
he still paced that ropeline's
Credo of semicircle: backyard thorn bush, sidewalk-edge to stone bench, left
  yard piss-soaked litter of pink azalea blooms.

502.3

I have nulled-and-voided, Lord. I have mis-
and de- and over- believed.
Half-prayed to 'Oumuamua,
not-comet not-asteroid, halo-
less, coma-less, elongated and tumbling
here out of Lyra constellation,
whose name means *a messenger*
from afar, arriving first
whose 'orbital eccentricity' exceeds
our sun's escape velocity.
Eccentric strayer: glottal
stop's half-choke be

the incipient of thy name.

502.4

Lapsible: liable
at any time to stray.
Lord, I have *harbored* my doubt
as in: moored there.
Clove hitch, taut tether, cleat.

502.5

Onamata: Greek for *names*. "The word comes
to designate language as such,"
"the audible icons of the divine"
says the *Dictionary of Spiritual Terms*

I've been Lent-praying-through.

Onamata, domiciles of the
utterable.
The credible.
If words were to lapse, if names were.

Announce themselves and quick-vanish, like 'Oumuamua.
Messenger from Afar, arrive first.
Your name, Lord, Your *onoma*, from the unburnt scrub bush: I AM THAT I AM.
Say unto them, I AM is my name.
Ehyeh asher ehyeh. Ash at its unburnt core.

502.6

To be in Time is called
to lapse.

Expose me
in time-lapse, Lord, one frame a second,
and watch me in 24 frame-speed, slow-filmed then sped

and lapsed clean out of Time.

502.7

In memory's jerking time-lapse credendum I stand

hard-of-belief and tugging
at a tether I'm untethered-from,

crabgrassy edges of Doubt's
thin shadow as it passes and I'm
grazed
barely by its ragged hem. I would
touch it again (Thou: help) I believe

I believe.

Little Faiths

o ye of little faith
   –Jesus of Nazareth

I

Forgive me I have wandered again off-
trail far
into the words

de-
nominated,
improper nouns

properly named

after neologisms

Solitary and solecistic,

riven by denominators
and split syllables
and monophthongs'
pristine vowel sounds,
wholly incorruptible

idioms of inarticulation

Pursuant to and whereupon and inasmuchas and whither

I have been assigned to worship
in such a way

outside the temple
(*pro*
fane)

as always I am

holy-garbed
garbled

What is its worth

The syllables' vowel-nucleus'
all-windowed hermitages

Who bows there over what illegible Latin vellum

What manner of prayer
is this so inhabited
by atemporal
tenses
unconjugatable

Little the faith that lasts
unless strayed
from sobeits and propositions and amens

and sense
you will not find me
in

I of little
faith

speaking worthship's argot

numinous, strangulated though it be

II

If he has cast his spangled lure
("durable & 400-times-
more-scent-dispersing")
into a cove

narrow and silent and stood there

dawn to noon dawn
to noon and felt that
insistence as itself

an act of faith, incontrovertible,

like a noun with no recognized
antonym—

& if he's felt that ghost
shrimp jig
he bottomfishes with
20-pound test line 70 feet

deep come

to supplant the kelp greenlings
he once meant to snag

as if lure might
replace the lured's

brown mottle in a skin of gold
why must we

voyeurs of this
dreamscape's allegory
be given
access to a cross-section

Fishfinder sonar

side-view all the way down
the semiopaque agitated
and utterly fishless sea

III

With the rough
tenderness of weeding
a strawberry thatch, touch

me thought by thought

You who Are and know You are

Blood-rinsed bowed and knelt-to

the vetch and melancholy and the bloody dock
self-propagating minute-dread
of what comes next

comes next

Yank claw loose then tamp
back into wet earth the long
straying runners snarled
in bindweed

The garden book says the runners drain the sweetness from the fruit
in their hankering after some other
richer soil some other less-
occluded
sunlight shaft

some anxious morrow-thought

(I language-thing am paraphrasing
parabling now) internodes

craving a future
a colonizing and seceding mother plant

I doubt You Lord but only
the way I doubt
myself a Thinking Thing

sending forth its nodes of incredulity

away from the plump and cloven burst glistening fruit before me

What is it to be *saved*,
as in *unspendable*,
hoarded for the not-yet and unusable?

Unmakingly I hereby set my hand
Res Cogitans Thought-Thing
doubting the undoubtable presence of mind and You

prayer-answerer, dethinking delanguaging You

O reign of matter
As is said in the *Corpus Hermeticum*
Naught is there which You are not

Who am I
speaking

Surely there won't have been
anything
that ever
I called *I*

IV: To a Reader

Whoever found your way here, go
on, go on, this is no place to dwell
among syllables and obfuscatory
wants that lurch and halt and fight
all unambiguous naming. Like a creek
self-purifying over stones
whose smoothness it creates
and then commends. Does
meaning sometimes disgust you,
its indefatigable advancement,
swerving around boulders and stormdowned
trunks toward the closural
opening of the mouth? Ambition's
background-running and obsessively
secretly self-correcting program, preoccupied
at every moment by all the ways we may
have accidentally and embarrassingly erred.
Already the latest findings
excise the former, in a redacted
blackout of the previous certainties.
Regardlessly, and purposelessly, be
well, be well, be well, Stranger. Sit here
these five-hundred-syllables-while.
If there were such a verb as *to bewell*,
bewail's near-homophone and antonym.

If there were such a name as Antonym,
a noun as *ante*nym—before the word,
and *of* it, as of a place, a time, a here, a this,
random and deictic Little Squalicum, high tide at 5 p.m.
as of
a faith, a little one. Which chooses
to last by rooting itself
intractably among Coke can and gull feathers, bark-rip
off driftwood, and hollowed-out crabshell,
and words. *Hi, I'm Faith:* windblown voice-over,
surfsuck's precatory bewailing, and
seaweed hung strand by strand over branch
as if deliberately to dry. Go on, go on,
say more to me, Wanter. Hold
your opinions like a crystal figurine,
antique and precious and precarious. Wild blackberries
cling under the four-lane's overpass.
Overpast would be a better name for memory.
That's an antiquated and precarious opinion. Bewell,
bewell, dwell
a brief while here, anonymous
and casual visitor, Antonym, implacably resistant to all name.

NOTES

In "Loathsome Repetitions," "I cried unto the Lord with my voice" and "Refuge failed me, no man cared for my soul" are from Psalm 142; "My soul is like earth without water for thee" is from the next psalm, 143.

The title "Disconnected Limbs Wandered Seeking Everywhere for Union" is from one of the fragments of Empedocles. "The Teacher" on page 33 is Aristotle, and the allusions are to his texts *Generation of Animals* and *On Truth*.

In "Not Easily Pulled Asunder": Thank you to Bruce Beasley, the prominent abstract sculptor, who's not me and shares my name. This sequence attempts to recreate through linguistic and poetic structures some of the complexities of his sculpture "Tenacity," reproduced photographically before the sequence, beginning with the word "ten" embedded in his title "Tenacity."

ACKNOWLEDGMENTS

My deep gratitude goes to the editors and staff of the journals where the following poems first met light:

Field: "By the Road of By and By"

Georgia Review: "Outside the Realm of Unconcealment"

Indiana Review: "Disconnected Limbs Wandered Seeking Everywhere for Union"

New American Writing: "The Paradox of the Heap, in Heraclitus's River"; "Little Faiths" [Forgive me I have wandered again off-]

Plume: "Called to Lapse"

Seattle Review: "Not Easily Pulled Asunder: Ten for *Tenacity*"

Subtropics: "Verily" (as "The Responsive Amens")

32 Poems: "Will"; "Little Faiths" [If he has cast his spangled lure]

I am deeply grateful to Luke Hankins and Orison Books for the vision of the press and for your support of this book. Thank you to Carol Guess for inviting me to two wonderful writing groups during the pandemic during which many of these poems were first conceived or drafted. Likewise to Luther Allen for convening "A Spiritual Thread" along with me, Dayna Patterson, Jennifer Bullis, and Susan Alexander, a collaborative project that led to "Outside the Realm of Unconcealment" and "Called to Lapse" (and thanks to Dayna, Jennifer, Susan, and Luther for the great inspiration of your poems). I'm thankful to the sculptor Bruce Beasley, for his work and for granting me permission to reproduce his sculpture "Tenacity" here. My gratitude goes to Rosamond Purcell for granting me permission to use her stunning photograph on this book's cover. To Bill Wenthe for his precise, honest, and often highly generative reactions to early drafts, from this book and for decades of close readings before. To Chris Patton, for his friendship and for early close readings of several of the long poems here. For Suzanne, always my first and most trusted reader. And great thanks to G.C. Waldrep, Kathleen Norris, and Lisa Russ Spaar, for their work and for their generous time and attention to this manuscript and for their blurbs.

ABOUT THE AUTHOR

Bruce Beasley is the author of eight previous poetry collections, including *All Soul Parts Returned* (BOA Editions, 2017), *Theophobia* (BOA Editions, 2012), and *The Corpse Flower: New and Selected Poems* (University of Washington Press, 2007). He has received The University of Georgia Press Contemporary Poetry Series Award, The Colorado Prize for Poetry (selected by Charles Wright), and The Ohio State University Press/*The Journal* Award, fellowships from The National Endowment for the Arts and The Artist Trust of Washington, and three Pushcart Prizes.

ABOUT ORISON BOOKS

Orison Books is a 501(c)3 non-profit literary press focused on the life of the spirit from a broad and inclusive range of perspectives. We seek to publish books of exceptional poetry, fiction, and non-fiction from perspectives spanning the spectrum of spiritual and religious thought, ethnicity, gender identity, and sexual orientation.

As a non-profit literary press, Orison Books depends on the support of donors. To find out more about our mission and our books, or to make a donation, please visit www.orisonbooks.com.

For information about supporting upcoming Orison Books titles, please visit www.orisonbooks.com/donate, or write to Luke Hankins at editor@orisonbooks.com.